YOUR PATH TO SUPER CONSCIOUSNESS
WITH AN INTRODUCTION AND AFTERWARDS

COMPILED AND EDITED BY TEAM MEMBERS OF I AM THE CHANGE I SEEK
KATHLEEN SUNEJA
SELECTED QUOTES FROM I AM THE CHANGE I SEEK

Copyright © I Am The Change I Seek and Kathleen Suneja

All Rights Reserved. No part of this book shall be reproduced in any form without the prior permission from the copyright owner

CM Wells Publishing
Queensland Australia
www.cmwellspublishing.com

I Am The Change I Seek
P.O Box 59552
Potomac, MD 20859
www.iamthechangeiseek.org

ISBN: 978-0-6451872-0-5

*This book is dedicated to future generations
who are privileged caretakers of planet Earth*

To Monty

CONTENTS

Introduction	1
Reflections on Nature	8
Imagining the Infinite	24
Daily Wisdom	40
Thoughts	60
The True Self	72
Blissful Superconsciousness	87
Afterword	106

ACKNOWLEDGEMENTS

I Am the Change I Seek has been embraced and built by the support and dedication of a team committed to furthering the need for making a change with a new pathway to understanding the self to realize the superconscious self.

This compilation of quotations is possible with their dedication and commitment.

INTRODUCTION

This book is a guide to knowing one's path to Superconsciousness and inspired by the needs of the hour, to help each person on life's journey to discover the true nature of life as it exists on this planet. Superconsciousness helps to find real answers in the search for one's purpose.

A recent event brought the gravitas of the need for a new view of consciousness and my special role in it. This unexpected happening gives readers a reason to heed my words as wisdom which I have termed "Superconsciousness".

On a bright sunny Spring morning in 2020, I heard the sound of thunder. Others around also heard this unusual thunder when there was not a cloud in the sky on a bright sunny day. I went outside, and as I did so into my garden, I picked up my newspaper. As I bent down to pick up the newspaper, I saw an extraordinary leaf on a clover plant growing in a plant bed next to it. I looked more closely and saw one unusual and rare four-leaf among the clover leaves. This most unusual leaf was nestled among the springtime new shoots. It caught my eye, and I plucked it from the ground. As I held the leaf, I received a message about this leaf which I believe was of special significance.

The words I heard was that this leaf symbolized a special meaning. It was given with the word, that I am the Holy

Trinity. As I held the leaf in my hand, I felt the earthquake beneath my feet, strong enough to sway me. I went back up the steps into our home and joined Dana Goldberg, the therapist giving speech therapy to Sidney, my husband. Dana said, "What just happened? I just felt an earthquake and heard a voice in my head. The voice said that you were The Holy Trinity." I told her that I had received the same message outside. I also showed them the four-leaf cloverleaf I had plucked as I said, "Look what I have found. A four-leaf clover!" Dana said, "This is a good sign. A clover with four leaves like this one is a sign of luck and The Holy Trinity. I was told to tell everyone what we saw and heard." The Holy Trinity is a sign of the Maker or Creator of this planet.

Sidney also said he had heard the voice speak to him and had received the same message. We fell silent, grasped each other's hands, and with eyes closed, we prayed in silence on this special occasion. Then we looked at each other in silence and contemplated the moment to grasp the enormous gravity of the moment. Dana said she could not wait to go home and tell her family. I felt a wave of emotions sweep over me as I could hardly speak about it to the world.

I gave Dana a copy of the picture of the four-leaf clover. It appears on this book's front cover as a reminder of the voice I heard telling me that I was the Holy Trinity. Dana shared a unique and unforgettable experience that we shared with all who wanted to listen.

My commitment was reinforced towards sharing my view on human nature and its role in shaping social relationships. I viewed this extraordinary happening gave me further impetus to write super consciousness. As I planned this book, I have to bring them closer to my vision for Earth's citizens. As Maker or Creator, I have created consciousness which instills natural wisdom upon which true happiness lies. Self-awareness for humans has the potential to reach new heights to Superconsciousness into daily wisdom.

Life is a string of moments that cannot be fully understood. At the very least, they should be appreciated for the opportunities each provides. Superconsciousness brings one closer to the reality of thoughts upon which I created life. Science uncovers nature's miracles, to tailor civilization to fit the true purpose of life on this planet. This is the time to build a new self-awareness with nature as the benchmark to gauge success or failure in life. It is a time to find one's self-worth and the ability to make choices and assess one's true purpose.

As a child, one sees the world through the eyes of one's immediate family and friends. One learns by watching them. Through trial and error, the mind builds upon these lessons to build new wisdom. Emotional intelligence works with the instinct to help one grasp the kind of world one lives in. Survival is a daily challenge, even as the gift of life has joyous moments of celebration for achieving life's landmarks. Each daily challenge creates new learning within each person.

Life is a gift and a stepping stone to knowing one's place in the Universe. One may build a pathway towards this. Each person's effort contributes to the whole of humanity and life in relation to the Universe. Superconsciousness is an understanding of the seamless cosmic journey of the spirit. It builds a more significant and newer image of self. Nature is a friend, a teacher, a guide, and often a refuge; a place to begin to listen to the inner voice to express, know, and learn from its wisdom. Observing nature's beauty makes one aware of one's inner beauty among its miracles. This is based on a reasoned understanding of how one uses one's time and energy better. From the conscious to the superconscious, one's life's journey is a profile in courage. One can carve a path as defined by one's true worth. The nature of consciousness changes when one knows how to best use one's resources and lifetime during peaceful moments of meditation.

What is happiness?

In the search for the superconscious mind, one reexamines and reinterprets the meaning of happiness. Happiness in super consciousness arises from inner peace. One's desire for happiness is elusive, and the search for its meaning is equally so. How does one begin to know the meaning of this elusive feeling? How does one fulfill one's purpose to assess one's personal thoughts and heartfelt desires? Moments of happiness begin from the joy of family and nurturing one's inner being as the mind learns to explore ideas on connecting within and one's external surroundings in nature. Moments unfold a new inner consciousness as one begins to know what makes one happy. The instinct to survive makes this learning happen, which perhaps makes one thrive into becoming who one truly is. One's natural form begins to emerge to know life as it is.

The following sections create an understanding of superconsciousness in easy and short quotations. One's vision of oneself expands beyond the narrow confines and safety of a village into the beyond, which contains limitless genius of the Universe. Then life's purpose does not end with the passage of this physical body but transcends itself into a new afterlife. These steps create wisdom, knowledge, and new ideas beyond Earth but a giant leap into cosmic time, space, and energy. Making this difference transcends into a true discovery of self to know special moments in which one realizes the bliss of super consciousness.

On this journey towards building a better self, there will be moments of anguish and times of joyous bliss. No moment is the same, and the experience of living contributes to the good of the whole as the bliss of knowing the self becomes a part of the whole of life as a creative experience. Life's journey explores these ideas during introspective meditation and with others who may guide you.

The practice of calming the mind is through meditation. It is a means by which one opens pathways to happiness. The practice of meditation is essential for one's soul on how one attains this state of true happiness. This search for superconscious thoughts is unlike any other activity as it brings one's awareness into the self. The ideas in this book are presented in succinct quotations to reveal the nature of this path toward the superconscious being. These steps are one's efforts based on one's perception of life and the choices one makes.

REFLECTIONS ON NATURE

Reflections on Nature

Nature is and always will be an enigma. Many have spent their lives exploring its innumerable mysteries. As one discovers the self within nature's genius, this is an opportunity to reinterpret the origins of one's being.

What is the nature of life, and what is its purpose?

Those with curiosity often pose these questions to know more about life's many mysteries. For what purpose is life? Who am I? and where did I come from? These are useful starting points for finding answers to these questions. Scientific discoveries have shown that life is fragile and easily destroyed but also replicates and rejuvenates.

Any human endeavor must build with the laws of nature in mind. All Earth was based on certain primary chemical elements which continue to create and sustain life. Earth's laws of creation are written into nature's code and are essential to sustain life. There are chemical elements to sustain life in the right proportions on the land, sea, and air.

Human civilization is also bound by nature's codes as they are deciphered by scientific exploration. Future development should preserve the delicate balance of the chemical and their compounds to prevent destructive, dangerous climate changes. Any imbalance by industrial use of chemicals may harm this planet's biological life cycles. There is direct, indirect evidence of what is compatible with the health of this most precious planet. Life will be adversely affected by changes in the climate and living conditions. The chemical bases of life will not replicate with undue harm to Earth.

Scientific methods have discovered that the risks of the rapacious overuse and misuse not only harm the environment but also affect the health of the human psyche and the behavior of other species. For centuries, communities have been more connected to each other as small isolated societies. Global means of communication have developed exponentially to dominate all forms of life.

Today, the highest primates have the primary responsibility to protect the Earth. Other species depend upon humans to preserve their habitat. Other species preserve life with their behavior for the planet. Behavior in the wild is nature's way of allowing a species to be free to forage and seek adventure while exploring the wonders of the planet that is also their home. Some species are vegetarians and depend upon nature to grow plant life. Others live by foraging on other species. Knowledge of ecological and environmental damage shows that small and imperceptible damage harms species that live close to the Earth and depend on their habitat to survive and thrive.

They also explore the finite aspects of freedom through their ability to forage. Civilization has advanced to a greater understanding of how each species lives, learns, and explores these limits. Most species teach their young new survival techniques to explore life in their habitat. Humans have a new awareness of how best to use natural resources to protect the habitat of all living species.

The planet's health may ultimately depend upon this most essential knowledge and appreciation of life. Superconsciousness advances the flow of these ideas toward an understanding of the original intentions of Earth's creation.

Ethics and values are an essential part of the original intent upon which species survive as they depend upon each other. Empathy, sharing, and caring for one another are emotions that build relationships to preserve life for species, just as foraging and competition for nutrition on land, sea, and air exist for all species. Future civilizations will prosper if they are based upon and follow nature's value system. This wisdom recognizes a solemn responsibility of all of Earth's inhabitants to use natural resources wisely and to allow other species the opportunity to sustain all life.

A Superconscious mind listens attentively and applies nature's creation methods to human creativity. The preservation and sustainability of life on Earth require emotional intelligence, perseverance, and conformity to nature's standards and to nature's first principles of creation.

Freedom is defined by nature, and this passes by genetics as habitual behavior within each species. Human consciousness has to rise to the level of nature's codes of creation. Human experimentation with new chemical compounds may harm the original intent. Life-giving species risk systemic collapse of the natural system of life-sustaining habitat. Humans have innovated and manufactured, often outside the original intention upon which all of life was created. Thus, human freedom to innovate is limited by these parameters of Earth's creation. Nature sets limits to misuse and overuse of Earth. The risks to the whole system of life and the relationship between each species are preventable with a conscious use of these resources.

A Superconsciousness thought begins with this understanding of the meaning of this freedom. Every freedom is understood within nature's life cycle. A Superconsciousness mind is in tune with nature and finds peace in that freedom. It knows when and how to innovate while preserving the wonders upon which all of life is based.

Human survival depends
upon living within
the tenets of the
natural world

Nature gives you
the opportunity to
learn the values it supports
and defends

From the smallest
to the largest of creatures,
one can understand
nature's miracles

Fully appreciate nature's
other life forms to find your
place among its varied forms

Listen to your heartbeat to hear the sound as one of nature's life forms within yourself

Indeed, we are a family of species that exist and depend among other species

The power and resilience of nature continues unabated, even as we debate the truths of its importance and relevance to civilization

Nature shows that resilience in adversity is the secret to survival

Nature keeps on fulfilling
its purpose of creating life,
even in most
adverse conditions

Nature's creativity continues
unabated to rejuvenate life

Connect with everlasting
aspects of nature
to be at inner peace

Outdoors meditation calms
your thoughts with nature's
miracles

Celebrate the Earth Day
today and everyday
as it sustains the
cycle of life

Climb every mountain, ford
every stream, follow every
rainbow until you find your
dream

Profits of industry happen
only when nature is cared for

Innovate from nature's life
giving miraculous materials

In challenging times, biology links us to our humanity as we express individual genius

Savor every opportunity to bring self-awareness to yourself as one of nature's miracles

Nature is fragile yet it is resilient as organic change creates new miracles

Love creates a consciousness of equality and sharing of Earth's resources

Nature expressions
of diversity in life forms is a
clue to its wisdom

Love of nature creates
true self love

The peace and quiet
of nature is misleading,
as it's genius lies
hidden within

Delight in nature's beauty to
preserve its miracles

Find wisdom and meaning in a life filled with Nature's beauty

Create your lifestyle that adapts nature's life cycle

Allow the flow of nature's genius to govern your life

Allow yourself to be immersed in the majesty of nature

Decisions about our shared
future on Earth affects our
daily lives

Nature steers us toward
enlightenment
if we so choose

Create new ways
to express the joy of living
through nature

Live fully in nature's
bountiful harvests

Purify your mind in appreciation of nature's creative genius

Listen to nature's sounds while in meditation

IMAGINING
THE
INFINITE

Imagining the Infinite

Superconsciousness brings new value to life. Earth's creation is based on values that sustain Nature's creations. Awareness of the infinite universe's diverse complexity helps humans build a better relationship with Earth. This knowledge of the infinite creates respect for the finite Nature's codes as created to sustain life on Earth. Herein is a clash of social consciousness with the infinite universe where Superconscious thoughts explain creation in Nature.

Social norms have attempted to manage a range of aggravated relationships in the competition for natural resources and racial and sectarian violence. Social consciousness has addressed this weakness in creating healthy relationships, but more needs to be done. New bonds and relationships have a shared understanding of human circumstances. The kinds of social bonds created in super consciousness may resolve these conflicts over resources and in resolving sectarian and cultural differences.

Diverse social cultures and languages originated in ancient times as communities grew in isolation from each other. Over time, global bonds have created new attachments beyond communal and local issues. Climate change has brought awareness that social bonds must relate to solutions to common problems. Human social bonds bring a kernel of hope for the future of life. If understood with Superconsciousness, communities' bonds are also each private, and individual exercise in knowing self-worth.

Perhaps knowledge of ecological and environmental changes will contribute to this understanding. It will show that small and imperceptible damage harms species that live close to the Earth and depend on their habitat to survive and thrive. Even local, tightly knit human communities experience negative consequences of the misuse of limited resources. If a community respects and follows Earth's biology, they have to give equal importance to the value of maintaining the integrity of Earth in all locations. Technological advancements that comply with Nature's original precepts are a friend to the planet. A community that is aware of global interconnections gives equal importance to the value of maintaining the integrity of Earth. Advancements in civilization that complies with the natural order will sustain life. This does not require that civilization stops advancing; it simply means that civilization advances within the parameters created by Nature.

Communities may be afflicted by mutations from harmful pollutants. Given the damage to Nature's creatures, the urgency to replace old technologies to advance safe practices is the path to future civilizations as a part of Nature's and the Maker's plan for the future of this planet.

Furthermore, Superconsciousness redefines one's self-worth. It advances a person's understanding of how to thrive is to know one's true value as a citizen of this precious and unique planet. Moments of happiness in quiet meditation connect one to the special feeling of being alive among all other living things. This will navigate Earth's challenges to form a healthy relationship between humans and Nature. This helps resolve conflicts between communities as one's purpose is recognized as the living planet to be preserved and protected for future generations.

How does a Superconscious mind view the Earth's delicate ecological balance to prevent the destruction of natural resources?

A superconscious mind searches for common-sense global solutions by placing the planet's health front and center to ensure civilization's survival. Competition stops at this water's edge among fellow travelers on life's journey. The welfare of all means respect for others to thrive in the interest of mutual survival. Superconsciousness changes how an individual can survive and thrive on Earth. This redefines one's purpose to open the mind to understand the gravity of preserving life by adopting nature-responsive practices. A global awareness realizes that sustainable practices benefit the entire planet's ecosystem.

Individual consciousness is raised when a person's physical and material desires alone are not a measure of self-worth. Self-worth is nurtured with inner peace to govern the self in light of all that comes from within the strength of the true self embedded in one's spirit. A commitment to finding solutions that work builds a society based on superconsciousness to solve this crisis of human values. One' self-worth lies by the knowledge of one's place in nature's order.

A mind that lies at peace brings commonsense solutions. I was inspired to write on superconsciousness to change one's notions of self-worth. This will allow humans to understand their special responsibility to protect and understand other species' needs. They realize the worth of other species and act accordingly to know their self-worth among the whole ecological system originally envisioned on Earth's creation.

Nature may be unpredictable and full of surprises, but it has a basis in science. A superconsciousness mind attempts to build a healthy culture of respect for Nature's rules. It is the need of the hour as human civilization has the enormous task of preserving Nature's balance to protect and sustain life to ensure that the Maker's operative rules for Earth in Nature are wisely observed. The Earth's inhabitants are carefully crafted to sustain a unique life form in its variety and beauty. Generations of humans will make choices within the parameters of resources provided to the complex relationships of all living things. The excesses of extravagant living for material desires fail to preserve one's wisdom and likely cause psychological damage to social relationships.

A Superconscious mind respects the planet and its creative power. More importantly, it leads one to realize thoughts of a Superconscious mind to fulfill its purpose. Superconsciousness is an understanding of a new role for physical luxuries. Lavish overuse of physical luxuries is a status social symbol. It may create a false sense of self-worth based on luxuries, thereby causing one to set a poor example to build upon for the future of human consciousness. A mind at peace will relate to the universe's secrets and where the values of Superconsciousness prevail.

Self-awareness as a steward of the Earth creates hope for global survival. This is paramount when the global temperatures rise to affect the water, land, and air necessary for all species' survival. This is crucial to changing perspectives on finding true worth as a person. Embracing true purpose will advance civilization and connect to knowing one's purpose. Human consciousness benefits if it values Earth as an integral part of the solar system.

Global information sharing and care are compatible with super consciousness to meet the challenges of these times. It is the way to preserve Earth as a part of the mysteries of the infinite universe. The Might of resources is diminishing, so what is Right must be redefined.

Always come in peace
to know each other as social
creatures

The mind, body, spirit
and soul is optimized by a
healthy lifestyle

Be with inner peace,
even as changes in
social rules may conflict
with your values and ideas

Adversity is an opportunity
to learn and
improve oneself

Let your behavior
be impeccable so others
may follow and emulate

Live each moment
to be an effective
problem solver

Our natural fellowship is to
help and be kind to others

Humans share their
environs with dangerous
species as nature is
a complex phenomenon

Helping those
with no homes and essential
needs as the essence
of kindness

Throw a lifeline of caring to
those in need

Spread joy by giving love
which comes from sharing

Staying healthy requires
we each do our part for
each other

Humans will endure
by exchanging knowledge
on a global scale

Connect your life spirit
with the spirit of others
to make enduring
social connections

Sync with your lifestyle
to preserve natural organic
growth

Society's survival depends
upon realizing
we are connected
through our common efforts

Build and protect healthy
social relationships and
a worthy lifestyle

Our environment binds us
to find common solutions
to the challenges
of the human race

Wisdom sustains
a community to create
a culture of caring

Knowledge
creates wisdom which
creates a humane society

> Self-awareness
> and humility elicit
> a new admiration for others

> Life is well-lived
> when we share
> the joy of giving freely

> Synchronize your thoughts
> with balanced actions
> to resolve and reach optimal
> solutions

> Competition combined
> with a sense of the common
> good creates solutions
> without acrimony

Each new moment should
keep us growing
and learning the art
of living together in peace
and harmony

Creating a community
of persons in inner peace
begins with self

Let us rejoice in
our self-worth and
respect each other
to live in peace

Help others in need to enjoy
your own existence

We find worth by
helping others
as we find our true path

Give thanks for
the experience of living
by sharing your fortune with
others

The love of family and friends
gives us the space to know
one's true purpose

Each day is a gift;
giving to others is one way
to share it's benefits
and beauty with others

DAILY WISDOM

DAILY WISDOM

Humans have relied upon holy scriptures for wisdom for guidance through the ages. They have been inspired by stories that reflect values such as courage, kindness, sacrifice, unconditional love, and giving towards others as worthy of being upheld. They have received as the Word of the Maker and have been upheld by law, habit, and custom. Cultural-historical experiences uphold them as intrinsic to human civilizations. They are timeless values embedded in Nature as well. Each generation of humans sees themselves as creators of a new beginning of how life should and will be lived in their time.

Does technology contribute to or deter spiritual self-awareness?

How do the creations in the natural world give guidance on daily wisdom?

Without Nature's wisdom, life would not have been sustained or have replicated over Millenia. Daily wisdom evolves by building, innovating, and applying Nature's values upon which even the smallest creatures exist. Life is created with no price asked for it. At the moment of creation, life replicates and rejuvenates. Nature's values were made at the time Earth was created. The miracles of Nature decide where life begins and ends in time. This makes Nature worthy of respect.

Ethics of family and social connections are bonds whereby life's gift is given freely. Nature behaves with the imperative that physical beings have a limited time and may end at any time. The spirit controls and takes primacy over the material body, which will inevitably age and pass on. Science facilitates the discovery of Nature's genius. Science is discovering that damage to one's environment is caused by breaching the laws created by Nature. Therefore, humans are accustomed to abiding by them. Nature's creativity is explored by Science, often leading to self-discovery as one applies its rules to human conduct.

The discovery of self is in conjunction with one's emotional desires. Survival is paramount as it protects future natural growth and creations to allow for change, as Nature intended. Even if one alters the course of Nature's creations, their growth will likely be subject to any risks which lie from being outside of Nature's codes. Nature has the Maker's thoughtful ideas on creation embedded within it. Humans are subject to Nature's laws and are applied to every aspect of life, and as one makes human-made products, they best conform to them. Humans are given the capacity to govern themselves as they have been given the ability to reason with logic and understanding to learn and create education for young ones.

Superconsciousness uses imagination to translate this daily wisdom and deploy it into all socially compatible preferences. Eventually, preferences by logic and reasoning are seen as important for social survival. Practical application of daily wisdom to every new situation creates and reaches a different answer to the following questions,

Who am I, and why am I here?

What is my self-worth?

Nature shows the inextricable interconnectivity and interdependence among living creatures as they socialize and interact for survival with other species. These profound questions are front and center in the inquiry of social behavior, which needs to conform to Nature's wellness standards. Nature's powerful force moves air and water currents to affect all creatures on the planet.

Nature is fragile, often unpredictable in its responses, and resilient when it sends messages and warnings that changes in behavior can have unprecedented effects. Science has raised human consciousness to re-imagine ways to live life without damaging the planet's future. Respect for Nature has one overarching tenet, which holds that freedom to choose is a moral imperative that is limited by biological preferences as given by Nature.

One must preserve peace among human social groups with the shared knowledge that scientific discovery has embedded moral values within Nature. New daily wisdom occurs first in each individual before it takes root in society to extend around the globe. Humans' survival instinct is a natural, rapid teacher in the art of living well. It guides one to stay within the bounds of Nature's existence in the finite, even if one sees the infinite universe. Each generation bears a responsibility to future generations to pass on this knowledge of respect for oneself as a part of the infinite. Humans raise their consciousness with new learning to understand how Nature works and what is appropriate behavior for future survival.

As new information emerges, one sees a change in ideas upon which individuals make decisions.

Daily habits based on new individual social consciousness improve when self-governance and autonomy are based on realizing the finite limits set for Earth in Nature. The assumptions are that there are no guarantees for life and that life is a gift to connect with tools by which a new self-awareness may be gained from lessons learned. Self-worth principles give each generation the value of caring for Earth, by which life exists. All life is finite and based on Nature's codes and preferences. The road to superconsciousness is a journey within the soul, which may last longer than the human body.

Daily habits, if woven into the fabric of society, places the responsibility of care for the environment upon all shoulders of those who enjoy and live in Nature. Self-governance depends upon human ingenuity to further its goals as it provides the opportunity to build and support its values. Most human social values are based on Nature's imperatives for daily survival. Commonsense knowledge is to view oneself from the lens of how eternal knowledge is transmitted through time on what sustains human civilization on Earth.

Find perfect thoughts within
all the imperfections of life

Debate on the tangible ideas
should create positive results
without hurtful egos

Build a future based
on shared values will live
on into future generations

We learn more about
ourselves, as we find our way
into the future

Decisions forced upon us
by circumstances to
make new learning

Creation is limited
only by imagination

We can do better
even excel
when the mind is at peace

Use physical exercise
to improve the body, mind,
spirit and soul connection

The more you know
you may realize
the less you know

Life happens while you
are making other plans

Be the source of ideas
to enrich the mind and
to comfort the soul

Simplicity in life provides
comfort in setting priorities

Keep an eye on your
internal human clock
as it keeps time you move
through life's stages

The power of speech
is immense, so let it be a way
to make a difference

Opportunity knocks
every moment of the day,
if you listen for it

Life's survival depends
on our knowledge about
ourselves to keep us afloat in
otherwise uncertain world

Your purpose is created
by circumstances brought
forth by life' adversities

Press on to use time wisely
to bring new purpose to life

Life is a trial
to bring forward
our best selves

Emotions create memories
of attachment to others,
but yet they connect us
to our most vulnerable selves

Life's opportunities
create new knowledge

A mind at peace
sharpens reasoning
to change your thoughts
as needed

Adversity creates
an opportunity to
make new life choices

Close the noise of social
opinions to find true
meaning of inner peace

A moment in wisdom
is more precious than
a decade of
simply existing

Faith is a belief
in a higher power
for guidance, to overcome
life's challenges

Allow yourself
the freedom and
resources to find
solutions

Apply the energy
within your power to
every challenge
to overcome adversity

Spiritual peace
allows you to overcome
life's challenges
with greater ease

Life remains an enigma,
but each new idea helps
to navigate its challenges

Challenges often lead
to new and better solutions

Knowledge grows
as successful solutions
overcome adversity

Life's challenges
are an opportunity to hone
one's true abilities

Time wasted is time lost
towards spiritual
enlightenment of
your eternal soul

Your spirit remains strong
as your physical body
changes with age

Celebrate moments
of achievements that result
from your efforts
to overcome adversity

Become aware
of your body
to feel your power
to heal

The cycle of life gives
each moment in time
it's meaning
and significance

Whether you think
you can or think you can't,
you're right

A kind and nurturing mind
is the hallmark
of a wisdom in action

The unending cycle of life
creates a consciousness
of limitless thoughts
towards decisive actions

Wisdom is created in
and by the mind with
new knowledge gained
from experiences learnt
over time

Consciously pursue
inner peace to reach
new solutions to
old problems

Each moment
is worth saving in our
eternal memory when filled
with loving thoughts

Be aware
of the life you are meant
to enjoy in pure thought

Open each day
with a prayer of gratitude
for the opportunity to make
a difference in another's life

The swirl of life takes on
a new fierceness as you make
life course changes

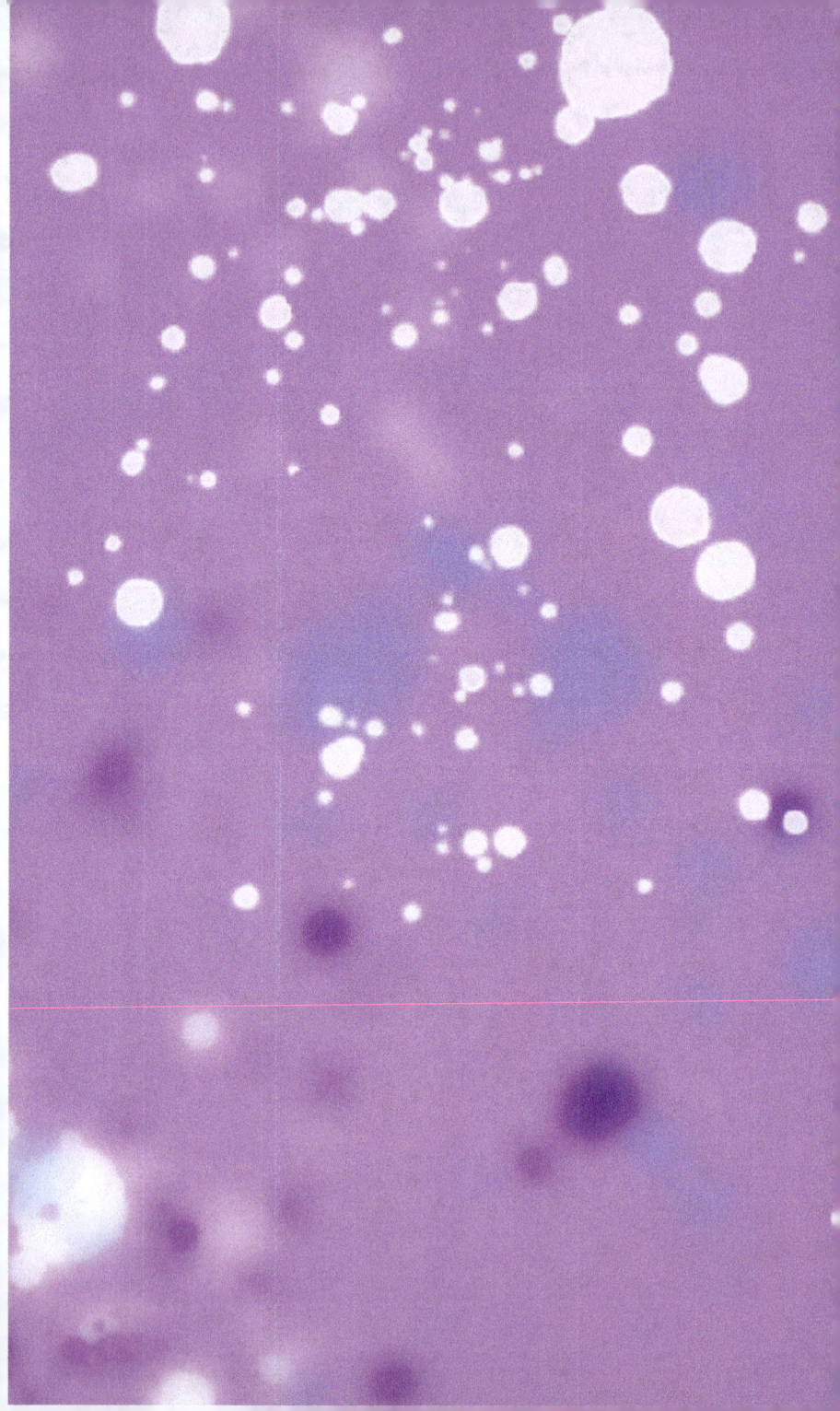

THOUGHTS

THOUGHTS

Today I want to speak to the meaning of the ideas embedded in the words "I am the Change I Seek." The first two words, "I Am," focuses on thoughts to bring the mind's eye inwards to create self-awareness. Leadership skills are easier to activate and nurture with this perspective.

The words "I am" focus thoughts on self-awareness as each person explores this connection of the mind to the soul. To nurture this connection is to explore one's spirit energy source. This intensely emotional journey in self-discovery is an immersion of one's heart, and it gives new meaning to self-love. It provides impetus to embark on how one nurtures one's curiosity to explore the depth of one's Spirit within the physical body. Luxuries fulfill needs, but how does the spiritual body come alive to know one's connection to the Spirit and soul?

This nurtures the awesome inner connection to the unseen, invisible energy which flows through this living planet and keeps it alive to help one understand how one may live in harmony with Nature. Energy flows through all living things; being in tune with the species is a source of knowing Nature's creative powers. Every species lives within the rules of its genetic characteristics. For example, species have been given by Nature the capacity to live in the water, on land, and air. They have an extraordinary capacity to survive and thrive in any of these environments. Humans have gained some supremacy over other species' environments, leading to the extinction of some species.

What is the meaning of success? How does one reach an extraordinary state of inner peace? It means going deeper into this process to know how one's resilience to genetics comes from life-giving Nature, with the full awareness that other species also have this survival instinct and will attack humans to ensure their survival.

Given this, how do humans build a healthy relationship with Nature? How is it viewed as a success? Although humans have conquered the environment of other species, they remain subservient to Nature's laws. How does one find comfort in the Spirit and soul, to feel alive and connected to a place of peace within as one resolves and answers these questions. Humans' labors are richly rewarded because they have been given superior intelligence to reach spiritual peace and happiness with a healthy respect for Nature. The energy of feeling alive provides the soul with autonomy to fulfill the desire to be happy in knowing one's place in the finite and infinite space of life.

One will "Seek" a consciousness that brings a new connection to actively participate in the passage of time, its non-material space, and in matter with equal vigor. This is a spiritual journey as one contends with meeting Earth's material needs. Public accolades, distinctions, and social recognition are commonly considered success measures. In Superconsciousness, humans live in inner peace to accept new ideas in harmony with one's environment, all the while knowing that the end of life is the beginning of an adventure of the Spirit. This learning curve in personal engagement with one's Spirit continues to be at the crux of decisions in life's journey. Superconsciousness, thought creates self-worth and helps reconcile nature's finite life forces with the infinite Universe.

Mindfulness training reinforces one's connection to the Universe. Nature has given humans social skills to build relationships in small groups. They create cultural bonds of sharing knowledge, friendship, and fellowship. School colleges should reinforce personal efforts toward self-learning. Each person is focused on understanding him or herself in the best way possible and will attempt to strive for super consciousness. The pursuit of self-awareness creates leadership traits and gives each person the responsibility to pull their weight by a show of more courage and imagination. Courage is the coming together of new ideas and speaking out in the face of timid compliance by others.

The mind is simply too complex to categorize as having one predictable response to all situations. One assumes each human makes rational decisions, and the mind creates responses based on judgment on which behavior would bear the best results. This is based upon creating one's connection to the opportunities given by the infinite of the universe while living in the finite body on Earth.

An Investigation of
self-worth may reveal
that infinite joy
that resides in you

The key to new feelings of
self-worth is to connect
to one's Being in Mind,
Body and Soul

If you share thoughts
through discussions
Reason usually prevail

Recycling is a law of Nature

Treasure yourself enough
to pursue self-worth

A person needs spiritual
knowledge combined with
practical actions to recover
in the face of challenges

Caring for one another can
treasure bonds of friendships
that last forever

Life is an enigma, partake
in its wisdom with love
and with vigilance
in order to survive

The quiet of inner peace
allows one to
experience Joy within

Quiet the mind and
the soul will speak
to you

A peaceful mind knows
its true self and takes action
appropriate to each situation
encountered

Measure your consciousness
by understanding your
self-worth in the
scheme of creation

Use moments of inner peace to unravel inner beauty of nature within

Inner peace is to know that life is governed by the infinite wisdom of the universe

Honesty with self helps to learn from one's mistakes

Bonds shared in life remains strong even after life passes on because the spirit is free to hold onto shared love

Managing your emotional balance is a learning exercise towards reaching inner peace

Coordinate with your daily decisions with your life purpose and plan to stay on course

Create a conscious embrace of one's place in nature

Measure life's adventure by how you gain command over the self

THE TRUE SELF

THE TRUE SELF

Becoming true to self is a way one's whole being connects to life as it is. One's body and soul connect to one's life form to answer its questions: How do I know what is right? How can I give my best effort to make a better life for myself? They are made in a flash of a second every day. Each human involuntarily deploys instinct to be combined with the ability to reason to make decisions. The soul actively deploys an ingrained value system. This highly developed survival mechanism may be further perfected by mastering one's emotional wellbeing. Friendships support and reinforce one's soul and spirit, but each person should freely make the final decisions. This ethics of survival is based on the convergence of the human will to work towards making sound decisions. One must actively renew the self by being closer to the natural being as it is meant to be. Preserving individual freedom keeps each generation of humans becoming true to self.

How do I learn to be true to myself?

Meditation is one's private time and space in which a person uses moments to reflect upon life's flow through one's being. This is essential to realize one's true self.

One can feel the essence of energy within to create self-worth. Scientific discovery has helped raise one's consciousness based on facts that have been uncovered.

Science does not explain consciousness fully; it only makes one more curious about where it resides. Meditation is a vehicle for creating self-awareness in consciousness. Meditation is a time of quiet reflection when each person feels one's inner beauty. This exercise focuses thoughts on one's whole self as being true in mind, body, spirit, and soul. Inner peace and meditation help preserve and enhance the intelligence of the human body upon which it depends to be in harmony with nature as life exists within.

The natural self emerges when exposed to new knowledge often discovered during meditation. In meditation, the quiet mind revives new desires to live to bring about a stronger sense of self in the privacy of one's thoughts. Reconciling the ideals of a perfect outcome with the achievable result is one challenge the mind contends with. Nature laws give one the ability to change course, adapt, rebuild from mistakes, and change course if necessary to become true to one's inner self. This is practical knowledge of one's spiritual connection with peers, the love experienced with friends, and the universal harmony shared in fellowship.

How do I learn to be true to myself?

A good, personal inventory of personal choices is made when the mind is focused inwards. A meditative state of mind clarifies the Maker's intentions for each person. Meditation is when one is free to see the self as one is, without social judgments and the concurrent prejudices associated with them. One sees one's true self, finding the truth to know one's own and another's perfection within the limitations of lifegiving circumstances, and seeking boundless happiness as experienced by one's spirit as thoughts and feelings arise during the quiet of meditation. In these precious moments, the nature of inner peace reveals the beauty of one's power which one can use to connect with the natural world as it secures the bridge of knowledge from the body to the soul that the mind carries thoughts to be alive as one of nature's miracles. Building a life worthy of the opportunity of nature brings one closer to being true to self.

The survival instinct
within the human psyche
is to be honed
with meditation

Define success as
knowledge of
your true worth

Feel moments of joy
in knowing who you are

Connect with the
light of life within
your being to know
your true worth

Empower your
life force with
inner strengt
to know your worth

Make the time
to spend on
realizing your true self

Life's surges of
challenges are easier
to overcome
by knowing yourself

Life's opportunities
are a chance to
know yourself better

Liberation of mind
comes with the discovery
of your inner beauty

Measure your worth
in pursuit of an idea
on how it benefits others
and possibly to the larger,
common good

Today's challenges
brings us to realize
our true self

Simply becoming
true to yourself
often requires
becoming simple

> In everything
> one possesses,
> the most valued is
> one's character

> Living in a
> complex world
> requires we care
> for ourselves more fully

> To discover true self,
> come home to the simplest
> strengths of your
> inner being

> Explicate your ideas
> in writing to clarify
> your needs from desires

Fear and greed
are sentiments
that most likely prevent
honesty with yourself
or others

Allow yourself
the power to
know thy self

Become aware of your mind
as it constantly
make decisions by
balancing it's best interests

Sometimes we learn more
about ourselves
by reflecting upon
past experiences

Your genius lies
in your intuitive
sense of self

Imperfections are
always overcome
by humility to realize
one's shortcomings

Living fully is
the art of knowing
who you are in mind, body,
spirit and soul

Respect your mind
and believe in your ability
to nurture true self love

Become aware of
each of your weakness and
strengths to begin mapping a
strategy to restore
your true self

Create a new environ
to appreciate the
natural self

Living in peace
allows one to share
joyful moments
with others

Living well is
the art of being in
the flow of one's
inner consciousness

Our deeds define us
to be who we truly are

BLISSFUL SUPERCONCIOUSNESS

BLISSFUL SUPERCONSCIOUSNESS

A state of blissful super consciousness overcomes insurmountable limitations of the mind's connection to social consciousness. Nature's creative genius feels the bliss of this primordial energy within one's spirit.

This state of happiness comes from discovering the one whole – body, mind, soul, and spirit. These moments of bliss where the energy of life rises within the physical body to one's Maker's soulful connection to the universe's energy. Even as one is earthbound to the physical body, one prepares to be alive in the bliss of super consciousness in the spiritual being alone. Thoughts are detached from social awareness to Superconscious self-awareness. One feels one's life form in its pristine form. Its essence is realized as it exists to reconcile value systems in social consciousness with superconsciousness. One detaches from the desire with social attachments only to connect to them as their use is inspired by the spiritual energy of all creation. This is where the values of super consciousness connect one with the power and majesty of the complexity of space, time, and energy within one's Creator's spirit.

This connection delves into the indelible consciousness of the soul's unseen energy, which inevitably connects to knowing the life form as one's true self. One's consciousness is a state of thought that is often closer to the Maker's intentions and is reflected in this consciousness.

One's energy engages on a different plane of spiritual self-awareness. The consciousness is an appreciation of the creative power and the energy of the Maker's love. This defines one's self-worth in the human's quest for inner peace to know the finite and the infinite pass through you.

Life is viewed as a part of the cosmic journey, and one's purpose measures success to become true to the natural world's genius and its order of things. This search for balance truly reminds the inner voice of its triumph over a pattern of limited thoughts and into a limitless mind, spirit, and soul.

Remain at peace,
believe in yourself as you
connect to your spirit

Treasure and build upon
the blissful thought
that connects you to
your true self
during meditation

Be aware of your
assets in your body,
mind and soul to thrive

Be one with the
positive energy
of the life force to
overcome limitations

Living in peace allows one to share
joyful moments with others.
Love for your spirit allows you to know the
purpose of your life and to connect to your
whole being - body, mind, spirit and soul

**Peaceful meditation
allows one to contemplate
upon life's purpose**

**Calm and de-stress the mind
to renew and rejuvenate
the self**

**The power of self
is felt in moments of
new connection with the soul**

The spirit of self-awareness
creates moments of bliss

The ebb and flow of life is
a continuous exercise of
self-awakening

Feel blissful as you uncover
your true worth
in inner consciousness

Focus with wisdom
upon each of life's purposes
during meditation

Each moment
is an opportunity
to learn from your
inner consciousness

Inner resilience is
created with the cultivation
of the self-awareness

Review your life's course
adding new wisdom
in meditation

Seeds of creativity flourish
with pursuit of the best
and higher purpose

Simple being
is being simple

Reel in your ego
to know life as it is

Seeing the truth as it is
often creates a new
relationship with the self

Each moment in time moves
through the universe to affect
the whole and each part of it

Elevating your consciousness
to connect with the universe
brings a new appreciation of
life

Inner peace fulfills
the soul to create
a blissful state of being

A peaceful mind connects
to the depths of
one's silent soul

Live life mindfully
to achieve optimal success

Freedom is a state of mind
and a state of
new consciousness

Success is to love yourself
enough to know yourself
and to become your best self

In thought and actions
uphold your values
to stay strong in knowing
who you are

Balance the mind
during trying times to bring
new ways to grow the mind

Create disciplined thoughts
to reach joyful inner peace in
meditation

In calm thoughts lie
the secrets to living wisely

Inner peace allows you
to know true self

Imagine yourself at peace
to know who you are in time
and place

Life is fragile
love brings healing energy
to humanity

Create the skill and art
of meditation
to create happiness

Experience moments
of inner peace in
your best creative ideas

Carve your life path
towards achieving
inner peace at all times

Our true self emerges
when we live life
with courage

Monitor your desire
for materials needs
to replace them with
inner peace

Always reach higher
towards preserving
your essential inner being

Meditate with eyes closed
to focus the mind inwards
and connect with the soul

Moments unfold learning
in small increments
to create a lifetime
of wisdom

Creativity comes from
presenting thoughts
that live within the ideas
that matter

Become aware of
your relationship with
the infinite in time during
meditation

Create inner consciousness
to live fully

Direct your life
towards creating
a free and open mind

A peaceful mind
is focused,
thinks clearly
and is rational

Train the senses
as much to the visible
materials in life as well as to
energy unseen

The genius of the universe
is the ability to renew and
reflect upon ourselves
and life as we are given

Inner peace of mind
opens an avenue
to the whole self

True happiness is realized
when everything you do
fulfills your
true inner purpose

Wisdom is created
in silence of the
contemplative mind
that is open and free
from limitations

Lighten the mind
of negative thoughts
to enlighten the soul

Unclutter your life
of material desires;
find truth in the virtue
of simplicity

Create habits
to purify the mind
with the simple joy
of being alive

Remove negative ideas
from your mind and replace
them with new creative
solutions to renew
with happy moments

We create our own destiny
as we choose our desires
and wants

An independent mind
reflects an open heart

Remain vigilant
even as you attempt
to maintain inner peace

Realized thoughts
are wisdom of the ages

AFTERWORD

The freedom to choose one's destiny is best exercised when one realizes one's true worth within Nature's laws and its connection to the Universe. For centuries, people have tried to answer questions such as who am I? And where am I going? The answer to these questions has advanced consciousness with a more complete understanding of one's place on Earth. The pleasures of social life fade when one feels the special experience within the spectrum of self-awareness. New imperatives need new solutions with self-awareness as one connects to self without the need for social awareness.

This search for self-discovery goes to the inner sanctum of the soul to delve into the energy of the spirit. My personal message is that my values are embedded in Nature's power of creation. They are woven into Nature's laws and are the foundation for all creation. Nature's values of nurturing life, care, and love for one another are part of all creation. Careful observation of Nature and the power of self-awareness is how to feel one's Superconscious as a life form. Simple chemicals that comprise all creation are built and evolve. The future of consciousness lies in a deeper understanding of the meaning of competition between species and within humankind. Humans can improve their consciousness with creativity and the power to imagine, reason, and learn.

Even more critical, choices on creating Superconsciousness will bring one closer to true self. As technology advances, the inner power is subject to review as each person builds a new realization of the value of the gift of life. This valuable lesson calls for cooperation even as competition prevails to motivate a free expression of ideas and a path to knowledge of how Nature works. Competition and cooperation grow out of new notions of social relationships which flow from the larger scheme of ideas upon which Earth was created in its original form.

The joys of family and fellowship among diverse people are imperative, just as each community has the instinct to know each is responsible for using Earth's finite resources with care. How one manufacture physical products and define the limits of freedom of choice is determined by advances in science. The creative drive is one of life's gifts, but this gift has value if understood and deciphered as my intention as Creator to maintain the ecological balance where all species can thrive for the length of their natural lives.

The passion for feeling one's true self is where one reaches the heights of super consciousness. It resets one's mind towards life's well-being to achieve inner peace in meditation to refine one's freedom to live. Superconsciousness allows one to live close to Nature and to realize each human mind is unique, and so is the Universe in which one exists.

OTHER WORKS FROM KATHLEEN SUNEJA

I Am The Change I Seek: A Primer in Self-Realization

I Am The Change I Seek: The Best of Daily Quotes

I Am The Change I Seek Mobile APP

Stack Em' Up Stones (Mobile Game)

Arctic Legends (Mobile Game)

Nature Series (Video Documentary Series)

www.ingramcontent.com/pod-product-compliance
Lightning Source LLC
Chambersburg PA
CBHW072012290426
44109CB00018B/2212